Copyright Notice

First Printing, 2012
ISBN-13: 978-1475205985
ISBN-10: 1475205988

Printed in the United States of America

Table of Contents

Introduction

Thank you for picking up your copy of Destroy Approach Anxiety by me Charlie Valentino.

Firstly, what is this book not about? Well it is not going to be a comprehensive pick up guide, detailing all the methods you need to pick up and sleep with hundreds of women. Those books already exist in abundance; some are great and some not so much. You bought this guide primarily because the phrase "Approach Anxiety" was in the title. This most likely means you've already heard of the term approach anxiety (AA) so I'm guessing you've already read at least a few books on the subject of "pick up" or "game!" Because of this I'm not going to waste your time by going over the same stuff all over again, especially since it's one of my beliefs that the overloading of information into our heads when we're starting out in pick up is one of the fundamental causes of AA.

What this book is! This book is primarily concerned with getting you over your first stumbling block having already entered the world of pick up. That is getting over your AA. But before you read any further, you have to understand and accept that you will have to get out into the field and do some work to get over this! That is your goal after all! So I'm here to make approaching beautiful women as easy as possible for you while you're starting out in pick up.

It is amazing just how many pick up books there are out there now. However I'm not aware of any books, good ones at least that deal with AA. Even the best pick up artists (PUA's) in the world started out at one time and they all had AA at one point. So I'm hoping this guide is going to be a little unique on the other books out there.

So who am I? My name is Charlie Valentino, I run a website which is linked to in the page above this one. I'm an author of other self-help guides for men, which you can find at the end of this book. I hope that proves my credentials, so let's move on to why you bought this book.

What Is Approach Anxiety?

We all know the feeling! You see a beautiful girl sitting on a bench, at the coffee shop, in the street, at the shopping mall or in a bar and all you want to do is approach her and say hi.

However we don't do this!

Why not? Because we're already thinking about what might happen if we do something socially unacceptable such as walk up to a complete stranger and start a conversation with her.

And once we begin to think about it, it's already too late! We're starting to make excuses why we shouldn't do it in our own heads just to make us feel better about not doing it. After all, there are some people around her now and they might overhear us while we're talking to her. Or maybe you should wait till she's off her phone. Perhaps you can wait while her friend goes to the bathroom so you can be alone with her. If you're at the coffee shop, it's far too awkward to talk to her while you're both in line, so you'll do it instead when you're seated...as long as she sits somewhere away from other people that is. Besides, you don't look your best today, you left the house in your bad pair of jeans and your trainers aren't as clean as they could be, so it's ok if you don't approach, tomorrow you'll wear all your best clothes to go out in.

But now she's leaving and you know you're going to feel really bad for the rest of the day! Was it really worth not approaching her? Especially considering you can't even remember what the excuses you had at the time were! And guess what? Tomorrow you'll do it all over again, only with a fresh set of excuses.

I'm sure all this is familiar with you! It's common and normal. After all approaching hot girls we've never seen before is not something we grew up doing every day. It's not like talking to Mum or going for a walk, but instead it's more like jumping from a plane or speaking in front of a large group. However, just like learning to drive, by doing it often enough you'll naturally transition from being nervous at first to being reasonably confident and competent.

Symptoms of Approach Anxiety

I'm sure you'll recognize the following symptoms from the last time you were debating making that approach:

1. Sweaty palms
2. Watering eyes
3. Heavy heart beat
4. Faster breathing
5. Dizziness
6. Sick feeling in your stomach
7. Feeling of nerves and discomfort
8. Paranoia that everybody is staring at you
9. Terror
10. Shaking voice
11. Trembling hands
12. Fidgeting
13. Making excuses not to take action

Why don't you write all these things down on a sheet of paper and show them to a friend! Ask him what he thinks these are symptoms of!

It could be anything in truth! They are also the exact same symptoms you'd get right before jumping from a plane or right before your first ever driving lesson, or taking your driving test for that matter. These are the same symptoms you get right before taking an exam or while you're being threatened by somebody larger than you.

So what does all this tell you? It's simply the symptoms you get while you're about to do something that's unfamiliar. That's all it is! Because you haven't before made a public speech you'll have those feelings, so the only way to combat them is by making more and more public speeches until it becomes easy. Or in our case we need to approach those hot girls until it becomes second nature.

"The only way to expand our comfort zone is to live outside it!"

They are the symptoms of fear! We get them as a self defence mechanism from when we were living in caves and hunting for our food. When approached by predators such as lions and tigers; if we didn't get these symptoms we'd be eaten alive. So we developed these fear reflexes over time in order to prolong our survival. If we rightfully felt fear when faced with a huge slobbering bear, we'd know not to try and fight it.

The only problem is, now that we don't hunt for our food anymore, our sense of what is fear, real fear and danger has been skewed. We get the same symptoms when faced with the prospect of approaching a beautiful girl as our ancestors received when trying to catch their dinner to stay alive.

But don't worry because we can change the way our brains perceive this false fear simply by training it. Simply by making a few approaches, our brains will soon realise this fear was completely irrational. After all, what's the worst that can happen from approaching a hot girl?

I'm sure you've heard all this before too! All you have to do is make a few approaches and it'll get easier from there. That's true, it will do and you should focus on that end goal of approaching girls being so easy that when you see a girl you really like, you'll be able to speak to her without any problems.

But hang on there Charlie...there's just one problem! How on earth do I make those first few approaches in order to get to when it becomes easy?

Well that's what you're about to learn!

What Are The Causes Of Approach Anxiety?

There are a few main reasons why we have approach anxiety, the fear of walking up to that hot girl. Sure I could just go straight into the section on how to beat approach anxiety, but by knowing the root cause in the first place, at least your own route cause then you'll much more effectively be able to combat it. So absorb this chapter and decide which are your main causes for AA so that then you can apply the correct interventions based on your own situation. Here they are below:

Irrational Fear of What Could Happen

Remember the analogy above about our caveman ancestors who developed instinctual fear to help them stay alive when faced with real dangers. Well yes, this feeling of fear has over the centuries been skewed since we no longer have to hunt bears for food. We now get this feeling of fear when having to do something we're not used to doing; approaching a hot girl for one.

Just like our ancestors did, when this feeling of fear enters our heads, we get the same symptoms as I described above and those symptoms we associate with danger and even death.

This is of course ridiculous because there is no way we are going to die or even come under any physical threat from walking up to a girl in the shopping mall and striking up a conversation.

We need to train our brains into believing this! Unfortunately, the only way you can train your brain to do anything, is by actually training it. That is to actually make an approach. Actually, by the time you've done about 20 – 30 approaches, that should have been enough for your brain to disassociate the feeling of approaching with the feeling of fear.

Don't feel bad for having this irrational feeling of fear though. But that is exactly what it is, irrational. People are a lot nicer and a lot more friendly than we often give them credit for and I'll give you an example with the help of a famous study.

In New York, a group of sociology students walked up to commuters in a busy subway train at rush hour and without any explanation they asked people at random "Can I have your seat?"

How many of those people asked, voluntarily gave up their seat? A huge 68%!

Now assuming the students weren't outright threatening those poor commuters for their seats, that's pretty impressive. I also know for a fact, though I have no numbers for backing it up, that if the students had have routed or given a reason for wanting the seat they could have increased that number to the high 90's!

This is because when we give justification or reasons, people are even more willing to "help out!" And it matters not what the justification is! For example, you could ask somebody on the subway for their seat because your feet hurt or because you're carrying a lot of bags. This would make sense! But how about if you asked for somebody's seat because it's your birthday next month or because your middle name is Steve. I can guarantee you, in the vast majority of cases you'd still end up getting that seat!

People are robots! Just like we are programmed with fear, they are also programmed to comply with requests as long as they are delivered with authority and confidence. People are programmed to be friendly and accommodating. People are programmed to go out of their way to be nice to people. When you provide a justification, your success will go through the roof!

This is one of the reasons I go direct when I make my approaches because it's easier to root and give a justification for.

Have you ever marched straight up to a hot girl in the street and said "Hey I just saw you from over there and I thought I just had to come over and say hi, because I think you are stunning!"

I say this with complete confidence and belief! But because I also give a justification ("because I think you are stunning") I am always, always, always met with a friendly girl who is willing to go out of her way to accommodate me!

So your fear is completely irrational, but you'll soon realise this as you do more and more approaches.

Learning Too Much Material

Now this is a big reason we get AA for a reason you may not realise.

Firstly and I'm sure you've heard many of the PUA gurus talking about this, when you're busy reading book after book, forum after forum for that magic PUA bullet that's forever going to answer your prayers and make approaching easy for you, you're not actually out there approaching any women.

Again, you'll be out in Starbucks enjoying your coffee and you'll see a beautiful girl that you should really be wanting to speak to. But you'll talk yourself out of it, because once you've read your NLP book and then your book by the next PUA guru, you'll be all set to start making your approaches. So you'll feel better because you've got an easy excuse not to take any action. Even though you already know more material than 99.99% of the male population!

I've done this before! I put off taking any action until I'd finished my new pick up book. Then when you finish it, you go over your other book one last time. Then you buy another new book on body language to perfect that. Then you go back into NLP in the hope you'll be able to make your approaches after reading your third NLP book.

Stop!!!

What are you after? A PhD in PUA studies?

And what good is any of this material actually doing you in all honesty?

Sure it won't harm you to actually know good body language and to have a structured pick up set in your head but do you think these things really matter when you're starting out and you've a million things rushing through your mind all at once and all while chatting to a hot girl?

Look, I want you to do this for me. You see that hot girl over there? I want you to go over to her right now. That's it, make your first ever approach right now! Don't forget your indirect opener, then your transition, all the while you need to make sure your feet are pointing slightly away from her, make sure your shoulders are in the right position, ensure you're gesturing the correct way with your hands, project your voice right, maintain eye contact, but not too much, have you got your demonstration of higher value (DHV) story ready to build attraction and then your DLV story to show her you're human after all, don't forget your kino routine, all the while you're doing this you must ensure you're somehow using your beloved NLP on her and yourself, don't forget your long list of negs you'll need to use if she seems a bit too cocky, whoops did you use a time constraint when you first approached? Don't forget to cold read her and tell her her fortune, remember to be cocky and funny and to make her laugh, finally don't forget to walk away without her number and if you can you should go for the kiss close!

I mean really! Is there any wonder why we have approach anxiety with all that useless crap spinning around in our heads and all while we're under pressure and scrutiny?

Getting over your AA should come before any of that crap! I guarantee you if you're reading this book, none of it will work while you're shaking and trying to think of what to say anyway.

What you need to do is forget everything you've ever learned. Get over your AA first and then any of the above will be a bonus for you once you're able to approach girls and start talking to them with confidence and with a clear head and have fun in the interaction.

All that crap is what will forever stop you from approaching because you're striving for perfection before you've even made your first approach. That's impossible!

I myself got over my AA simply by keeping things simple!

Simple!!!

For me the direct game is the most simple which is why I always use that!

There's no crap flying around my head, no routines I need to remember, it's just me and her! The real deal!

And it works!

But more on that later!

Lack of Confidence

Of course you're going to be nervous when starting out! That's completely natural!

And I'm not going to lie to you, you at least have to look and appear confident to her for your approach to work well.

Confidence is the number one thing that women are attracted to in men. It's not looks, money or status, it's confidence that they love.

Fortunately we can fake confidence even if we don't have it. It's all about having great body language. I'll talk more about body language in a later section, or you could read my book Confidence For Men which covers everything in more detail. That book is linked at the end.

You should never expect to be fully confident until you are first competent. Remember the following formula for confidence:

Competence = Confidence

Remember my driving analogy earlier? You were nervous when you first got behind the wheel but you soon became competent and therefore confident at driving.

Approaching is the same thing!

Did you know that body language is the key to confidence? Take a look around you at your local bar. See if you can spot who is confident and who isn't. It's easy!

The truth is you can appear confident to people on the outside simply by how you are projecting yourself, your body language. But did you also know that having good body language actually makes you more confident? It's true, it works both ways round and I'll explain it in greater detail later.

For now I just want you to ask yourself if this is one of the reasons why you're not approaching girls so that then you can nail the correct intervention strategy which I'll give you later on.

Caring Too Much What Others Will Think of You

I want you to ask yourself honestly, do you care what other people think of you?

I'm guessing that in the vast majority of cases the answer is a big fat yes!

It is this caring what others think of us at any one time that stops us from actually taking action and doing anything. Talk about locking ourselves inside a self-imposed prison and then throwing away the key. Or worse still, we're taking that key and giving it to other people to hold, giving them the power over us. People we don't know, don't care about and will likely never even see again.

This was always a big problem for me. I'd see a nice girl in Starbucks and I couldn't get the courage to approach her because the room was full of other people, some of whom would see me stand up, walk over to her and start a conversation which they wouldn't be able to hear anyway.

If this is a problem for you, then it's a pretty safe bet it doesn't just effect your approaching either but other areas of your life also. I'm willing to bet there are times when you don't dare speak your mind to your group of friends or to volunteer your opinion at work in case somebody sat around you may think something negative.

It really does sound silly doesn't it! Caring or for lack of a better word actually fearing what others think of us is what stops us from actually taking action on many things, most of all approaching.

I want you to imagine that situation where you want to take action, where you want to go up to that girl and speak to her. You can feel something starting to brew in your head. You're thinking about it! You're thinking about what it will mean to make that approach to the attractive girl sat on her own, enjoying her coffee. Now you're wondering exactly how you should make your approach. Then right after that, you're wondering about any consequences of approaching her in front of other people, possibly what they may think about you. By this time, you're on the fence, on a knife edge trying to make the final decision about taking that necessary course of action. You're giving it too much thought! Then, finally the moment passes! The girl stands up and leaves!

Now how do you feel?

Do you feel terrible, like you've been robbed of an opportunity for personal growth? Or do you feel relief because in the end you didn't have to put yourself on the line?

Feeling either way is very common and normal. But the fact is you decided to give the key to your prison cell to others in the room, you allowed other people complete control over you, you are not in control of your own destiny.

We much prefer doing the easy thing which is doing nothing. But we both know that doing nothing is not an option if we're to start approaching girls and improving our lives.

And what of those people who were in the room when you wanted to speak to that girl? What of those people whose opinion meant so much to you at the time that it meant doing absolutely nothing. When you leave the room yourself and you go home and you're regretting you didn't take any action, are these people going to matter squat to you? Will you even remember them?

"What you think of me is none of my business!"

Terry Cole-Whittaker

She May Reject Me

Is this the reason why you're not making your approaches?

All the greatest PUA's in the world started out somewhere and they've all been rejected, many hundreds of times, and now that they are great PUA's they still get rejected.

So I'll be honest with you and say that yes, you're probably going to get rejected too, an awful lot in fact.

But you should never let that hold you back.

Of all the many times I've been rejected, I've never once come under any physical harm! I'm still alive, and now I'm writing books telling others how to not care about being rejected by a girl either.

In fact you should enjoy it! And you will enjoy it! Because you took the bull by the horns and took action when all the other guys out there are unhappy because they don't take action.

I'll tell you this as well. You're a million times more likely to get a positive result by taking action than by not.

I'll also tell you this. Those times I got turned down after making an approach gave me such a buzz, that what tends to happen is you're immediately looking for your next "target" and for whatever reason I can't explain, your next approach always, always, always goes ten times better than the one before. I think it's because you're on a high from taking action, the adrenaline is pumping through your body and the girls can sense this and they like it.

What's more is that, the adrenaline seems to kill your AA. Once you've made one failed approach during the day, or night for that matter, your AA tends to get cut to shreds. After you've made another approach it almost vanishes completely. You're buzzing from the adrenaline and things absolutely always go a heck of a lot better.

So you should expect to get turned down the first time, treat it as a warm up approach and if anything good comes from it then you must be getting good.

But let me tell you this. Even when a girl does reject your approach, that's all she's actually doing. She is rejecting the approach and nothing else. She's not rejecting you as a person. There's no way a girl can reject you as a person from an approach, she knows nothing about you. So never ever take a rejection personally. Remember that you're the only guy on that day, week or even month who had the balls to walk up to her in the middle of the day and tell her you think she's hot. You've just made her day in fact, she'll be on a high for the rest of that day and she'll probably even tell her friends that a nice, charming and friendly guy just hit on her in the street.

That's completely true though because even with the most attractive of girls, this happens so rarely that you'll make her day if you do it. You'll stand out from all the other guys that never do this, and you'll have her respect right from the start.

The truth is that girls walking up and down the street in their nice clothes that they went to a lot of trouble to pick out actually want to be approached by guys. They would welcome your approach, as long as it's done with confidence and decency.

In any case, you should not be making your approaches with rejection in your mind. You need to frame it as if you're deciding if you're going to take things further yourself and not the other way round. There has been many times I've approached girls and ended up not taking their phone number because we really didn't have that much in common or because they really weren't all that intelligent. You are the guy who had the balls to march up to her, so it is you and not her that gets to decide if you want her number, not the other way around. We'll talk more about that later.

Now onto the reason you bought this book.

Strategies for Destroying Approach Anxiety

We're now on to the reason you have purchased this book. If you've skipped the rest and have jumped straight to this section then I suggest you go back and read the rest. You will after all do much better if you know the reasons or in particular your specific reason why you suffer from AA so that then you can make use of the best techniques for getting over this stumbling block. We do after all suffer from AA for different reasons and everybody is different.

Having said that, the following techniques will work in the vast majority of instances, they have helped many people including myself. Feel free to pick and choose the ones you feel will be the best interventions for you, or otherwise try them all and you'll soon have no problems approaching any girl you desire.

Listen to Motivational Music

This is one thing I know works for the vast majority of people. Play your favourite motivational tunes on your iPod and you'll already be on a high when you see that girl.

I used to have a long list of great tunes that I'd always be listening to as I walked around my town. If I saw a nice girl I'd start my approach and take the plugs out from my ears seconds before I made my opening line. This made everything feel spontaneous, which it was and occasionally I'd even work the fact she'd interrupted my favourite song into my opener.

I'll say right here that I personally always practice day game and nine times out of ten I open with a direct opener.

"Hey, I was just over there and I saw you and I thought to myself, oh my god, you are stunning, so I just had to come over and say hi, or I'd be kicking myself all day...My name is Charlie", at this point we shake hands. "I really hope you're the friendly kind of girl because you just interrupted the chorus on (insert song title here)."

The best songs to listen to would be ones that have a personal relevance to yourself. Songs that hype me up won't necessarily be the same songs that get you in the mood. Having said that, I did do a lot of research on forums trying to find universal motivational songs and I did have quite a big list at one point. Unfortunately my hard drive got wiped and I lost a lot of them. However there are some classics that simply stick in the mind which you should download and have on your iPod.

Greatest Day – Take That

Believe – Josh Groban

Eye of the Tiger – Survivor

Gotta Be Somebody – Nickelback

I Believe I Can Fly – R. Kelly

It's A Beautiful Life – Ace of Base

It's My Life – Bon Jovi

March On – Good Charlotte (highly recommended)

You Gotta Be – Des'ree

Hero – Mariah Carey

Beautiful Day – U2

Nessun Dorma – Pavarotti

Affirmation – Savage Garden

Song 2 – Blur

Beautiful One – Suede

I Won't Back Down – Tom Petty

I Feel Good – James Brown

Tub Thumping – Chumba Wumba

One Day More – Les Miserables

My Way – Frank Sinatra

Everybody's Free (To Wear Sunscreen) – Baz Luhrmann

Go Your Own Way – Fleetwood Mac / Lissie from the Twinings Ad

Don't forget to add your own special songs to this list!

Look Your Best

This follows on from what I was saying earlier and that many of the excuses we create to make ourselves feel better about not approaching come from going out not looking our best.

It's so easy not to approach that hot girl because we didn't leave the house in our nice clothes or a decent pair of shoes or because we decided not to shave that day.

If we leave the house every day knowing that we look our best then there are no reasons not to make that approach.

But more importantly than that, if we look our best then we'll feel ten times more confident when making that approach. You really do need to leave the house every day feeling unstoppable and looking and feeling great is such a huge part of this.

There's not really much else to say about it other than; good grooming and dress well.

Another thing you should be doing as a more long term goal is to build a good physique. While women are not as into looks as men are, I'd be lying if I said looks weren't important. Building a nice body is very attractive for women but more importantly than that, if you have a great body then you'll feel ten times more confident than if you were overweight.

Approach in a Strange City

This may sound pretty silly but back in the day when I had really bad AA, one of the things that used to go through my mind was; "what if someone I know sees me get rejected" or "what if I see her again."

Thinking back to it now it really does make me sound like a wuss but it had a major effect on me at the time and I live in a big city. I can only imagine this would be worse for the guys who live in small places who really do have to make the most out of every approach and interaction.

For this then I suggest you travel two or three towns over, maybe even get a room for a couple of nights. Find your nearest big city that you don't call home and dedicate a few days to approaching girls in that city.

You can literally get turned down as much as you like and you'll forget about it within ten minutes, move on to the next one and nothing is going to come back to bite you later on.

Another benefit is, if you go to all that trouble; travelling to the city, getting accommodation etc., you're really going to be wanting to make the most of it by making as many approaches as you can.

Worship the Three Second Rule

When it comes to pick up, the three second rule really is the king, queen, prince, princess and all the aristocracy put together.

Remember the list of AA symptoms at the beginning of this book? They are your enemy and they will strike at times no matter how good you get at approaching. The only way to defeat them is by worshipping the three second rule so you don't give them time to attack.

You need to see the girl and already be walking up to her without thinking about it. It needs to be automatic! A reflex action!

So in order for things to be this easy, you really need to have a structure in your head, but it needs to be a very simple structure, which brings us to the next section below!

Keep It Simple

I spoke at length earlier about learning too much material; NLP, body language and every pick up book by every "guru" out there. Doing this really complicates everything and makes the whole process of simply walking up to a girl and talking to her a lot more complex than it needs to be.

When I used to walk round my town looking for girls to talk to, it was the lack of simplicity that was the largest cause of my AA.

When I decided to forget everything I'd ever read and just go direct everything seemed to fall into place.

Why do I love direct game?

Because it is so simple!

It's just you and her in the moment! There is no crap flying around your head, trying to remember routines or games while under extreme pressure. You simply tell the girl you think she's hot and then you get into a normal conversation.

Then and only then, when you've done several of these and you're on a high and you are over a large part of your AA should you then contemplate any of the tricks you've learned from all the other books.

Remember, first you get competent, then you get good!

I've included a simple direct day game structure near the back of this book for you to take a look at. It's the structure that I recommend because I know it works, but feel free to do your own thing.

There is though one stipulation to going direct during the day, and it's something I've already touched on a little bit. For direct day game to work to its full effect, you really do need to come across as being confident.

Which brings us to the next section.

All You Need Is Confidence

Ok, so if there's only one thing you need to remember and try and concentrate on while your head is spinning making your first approaches, it's to try and at least appear confident.

Confidence is the number 1 thing that women are attracted to in guys, whether or not they'd admit it.

Fortunately confidence is easy to fake on the spot with just a little bit of practice.

You can easily make yourself look confident by having positive body language. But the magical thing is, that by using positive body language, you do actually end up feeling more confident.

Really, you need to try it the next time you're talking to your friends. Use the tips I give you below and feel the change in your body.

It's easy to tell who's confident and who's not simply by looking at their body while they speak. You can even come over as being confident even if you stutter your words, as long as you have a confident body.

Did you know that when we communicate, the words we say have only 10% significance to the overall message we get across. A huge 60% of the overall message comes over through body language. The rest being a mixture of voice tonality, pitch and eye contact.

Try speaking to your group with your arms folded and see how that feels, never mind how it looks to others. Your body is being closed, so that's also how your mind behaves. When you open up your arms, you physically become more open yourself.

If the body has this much power over our minds, imagine what happens when you actually start using active gestures while you speak. You physically become more confident in the moment.

This is the secret weapon you should be using while making your approaches. Not only does it look good from her point of view, but it'll make you feel awesome as well. Follow these easy to master body language traits and make sure you use them when you approach:

Hand Gestures

Simply bend your arms at the elbow and make slow, small and comfortable movements. You can make them slightly bigger if you're emphasizing a point. You should watch TV presenters and see how they do it. They know how to draw you in when they speak so you should learn from them. Be careful not to overdo it, as this is quite easy to do. Get some practice in the mirror.

Widen Your Stance

Simply spread your feet a little further apart while you're standing. Confident guys aren't afraid to take up a little more space. This gives you a better grounding and your mind will know it.

Keep Your Movements Slow

Confident people don't get alarmed at anything. They are the complete opposite of erratic. Erratic people react to movements around them in case they are threats. Confident people don't! Simply keep all your movements slow and controlled.

Don't Cross Your Arms

We've already spoken about this! It's dead easy and very important.

Stop Fidgeting

Be honest with yourself if you're a fidgeter or if you have any nervous ticks about you. This will give the game away that you're not confident. So you'll need to work on cutting them out. Checking your watch or phone every minute is fidgeting, as is taking frequent sips of your drink.

Another important thing with confident guys and something you really need to have when you're making your approaches is complete belief in yourself.

For the girl to buy into your approach, especially a direct approach, you need to believe that you're one of the greatest guys walking the face of the planet. Trust me, if you actually believe this, then AA is probably not going to be a problem for much longer!

You're The Prize

I mean really, how many guys have the balls to march straight up to a hot girl in the middle of the day and tell them they are hot?

You're gonna stand out that's for sure!

So remember that you are one truly unique guy! You are the selector and you are the prize!

Because that girl you're about to approach is not going to get hit on in the middle of the street again like this for a long time. She knows it too!

So remember while you're making your approaches, just how awesome you really are!

You need to also keep in your thoughts that you're not approaching her with any goal in your mind. You may after all not even like her! Perhaps she's not too brainy or she smokes or she has no hobbies at all. You're simply going over to her to find out if she's worth getting to know a little bit more.

But that's up to you to decide, not her! Remember that! You are the one who gets to decide if you want to have her phone number. And if you choose not to ask for it, because she doesn't meet your standards then it's really no big deal is it!

Enjoy Being Rejected

Every time I've been rejected I still always felt great afterwards. This is because I knew I stood out, I'd still made her day and because I was buzzing from it, my next approach would always go ten times better.

There are a million reasons why you don't hit it off after an approach; perhaps she has a boyfriend, is married, just got out of a relationship or is from a different city. I've had it all. No matter what the reason is, there is no reason at all why you should leave in a bad mood, kicking yourself or thinking there's anything wrong with you just because you didn't get a phone number.

As long as you have fun whilst day gaming, that's the main thing!

I've always had fun in my interactions and normally the girl has had fun too. If you can leave her in a good mood, with a smile and a handshake then you'll be in a much better mood for your next approach, which you should try and do as soon after as you can.

Get A Wing

Getting a wing man, a mate who you can take along when you go into the field is one of the best things you can do to help you destroy your AA.

The best kind of wing man you could have would be someone who has the same goals as you and who is a few levels above you in experience.

A wing man can push you and make sure you do your approaches and not chicken out.

You can also push him and make sure he doesn't chicken out either, it works both ways.

When you go out with a wing, you feel obligated to make that approach, because if you don't it's not just yourself you're letting down but your wing too.

You can take turns in making your approaches and observe your wing from afar. I've found that by picking each other's targets there really is no way of backing out. If you've chosen a girl for your wing to approach and you wuss out of approaching his choice for you then you're really going to look bad. There's no option I'm afraid, if you go out with a wing, you're going to make your approaches no matter how terrified you are.

As soon as he picks one out for you, you need to already be on your way, just don't think about it, just go!

This really is great motivation and works better than just about any other trick.

You can even work your wing into your interaction to make it sound more spontaneous and part of your transition from the opener too.

"Hey I was just over there with my mate and I saw you and I just had to come over and say hi to see if you were friendly as well as stunning!" Shake hands, introduce yourself and gesture in the general direction of your wing, "now see what you've made me do, I ran away from my mate and now I've lost him, you'd better be worth it or I'm gonna be so mad!"

Weaving your wing into the scenario makes the whole thing seem more real and spontaneous.

Also if you're dealing with a two set (two girls) then after a minute or two your wing can, and should come over and introduce himself to the group. This takes some of the pressure off you and also gives you a chance to isolate your chosen girl.

Likewise, if your wing opens up a two set then you can make your move over to the already warmed up set and break your way in. This is about as easy as approaching gets because all you need to do is say to your wing "Hi, there you are! Where did you run off to?" Then your wing can simply introduce you to the group. Bang, you're in! Approach done!

Getting a wing really is one of the most important things you can do to getting over AA so I really suggest you sign up to a local PUA forum and arrange to meet up with somebody. Feel free to try out a few different wing men until you find somebody who matches your personality.

http://www.pick-up-artist-forum.com/ is a great place to start looking for a wing man, it's an international website but it has many spin offs and hopefully one for your local area.

Rewards and Punishments

Many people who suffer from AA play variations on the punitive punishment game. I've tried it myself although I've always thought there are better ways of going about it.

The principal of the game is that you give your mate, or wing $100 or an amount that will be slightly uncomfortable for you to lose.

You get to earn your $100 back one small portion at a time. So for example, he can point at your next target and if you chicken out of the approach, he gets to keep $10. So the amount you're playing for then becomes $90 of your own money.

The one time I tried this game in England, I ended up playing for £20 per approach. I handed over £100 to my wing at the start of the day. I lost £60 that day.

Sure I was gutted for losing the money, but at least I had made 2 approaches which was a lot for me back then. However, looking back on it; not approaching those 3 girls he told me to was not worth me losing £60.

Give it a try if you think it will work for you.

However, it has been proven that rewards work far better for motivation than punishments. How do we train Dogs? Do we punish them for bad behaviour or do we reward them for good behaviour?

So how about instead, you try the reward game!

What is your favourite food? How about you treat yourself to a steak meal at the best restaurant in town if you make ten approaches in one day? I can promise you this, that steak will taste pretty good knowing you've just destroyed your AA and you've a few new phone numbers on your cell.

Or perhaps you could buy that new iPhone you've been wanting for ages?

Playing for rewards instead of punishments means you don't stand to lose anything for not approaching. But you certainly stand to gain if you do!

Get a One on One Instructor

Finally, this last piece of advice for getting over AA is the coup de grace!

This is for those who really are suffering from AA and who really want to get over it and start approaching girls to improve their lives.

I'll tell you now, this is the route I had to go down myself!

I went to London about three years ago and paid a professional instructor £400 for two days of walking around the city approaching girl after girl after girl.

Put simply...It works!

If I had to go this far, not to mention travelling their and paying for accommodation then I had to make sure I gave it everything I had and I did!

For two days, 8 hours per day he would point to a girl or group of girls and without even thinking I went up and did it. I went direct every time and I just could not believe how easy the whole thing was. It really did give me all the confidence in the world. And now I'm here telling you to do the same thing.

For me, this really was a last resort, but it works better than anything else in the world at destroying approach anxiety. Why? Because I paid a lot of money so I bloody well made sure I got my monies worth.

At the end of the second day, I went to the best steak house in the capital and had the best steak I'll ever have in my life, knowing my life was changed forever.

I approached more girls in two days than I'd ever spoken to in my life. All kinds of girls as well from countries all over the world. By the end of it, the instructor, who I remain friends with didn't even need to point out targets for me, I was simply choosing my own targets.

When I returned to my home town, I simply carried on where I'd left off in London, it was easy!

You yourself may not need to go this far, paying an extortionate amount of cash for an instructor to push your limits and give you hell if you don't obey his commands. But sometimes, making that financial commitment, something that actually damages your pockets and your bank balance gives your brain that special shift it needs. After all if you spend thousands on a new car, don't you make sure you look after it to the best of your ability? You should have no problem with spending money on something that is going to alter your life forever and the more money you spend, the more uncomfortable the transaction is for your wallet, the more effort you'll be ensuring you put in, the more determined you'll be to finally destroy your AA.

I left my AA that day in London a few years ago! And it's never come back since!

I owe it all to taking action! And in any case, I made the money back since and looking back on the whole experience; it really was one of the best memories of my whole life.

Direct Day Game Structure

I'm going to go into this as briefly and simply as possible. Remember, the whole point of direct day game is its simplicity.

Spot her and worship the three second rule.

Make your approach; if she's walking then stop her at least 2 meters in front. You may need to angle round to do this but make sure you get in front of her giving her slightly more than enough room to stop.

Put up your hands, aiming at her solar plexus to get her to stop.

Make your opener. "Hey I was just over there and I saw you and I thought to myself, oh my god, you are stunning, so I just had to come over to say hi to see if you were friendly as well."

Introduce yourselves and shake hands.

By now, you should get an idea of how receptive to your approach she's going to be. Now also comes the most difficult part of the direct approach which is the transition. If you have a wing then use him as a part of the transition. All you really need to do is say something, anything at all so you take a little pressure off her. Remember her mind is probably spinning due to just realising she's being hit on.

Transition: "Haha I was just with my mate over there and I literally ran away from him when I saw you, I have no idea where he is now, If I lose him we're going to be having angry words!"

At this point if she has a boyfriend you're about to find out. However, it's often a test or an instinctual reaction. In which case if she says she has a boyfriend, I like to playfully say "you don't have a boyfriend!" This normally gets a laugh. If she does have a boyfriend then so what! Just be a normal friendly guy and ask how her day is going.

If she sticks around and is receptive, all you really need to do is get into a normal conversation. Try and avoid putting too much conversational burden on her at first, until the time comes when she starts asking you questions. This is the "hook" point when you know she's interested. After this you can ask her about what she does/studies at university or about her hobbies etc.

You're looking for common ground to try and decide if she's worth you taking her phone number.

That's it!

I'm not going to complicate this any more than needs be. Remember that first you get over your AA and then you can start using all the tricks and routines you've learned to try and build more solid interactions.

Final Words

If you've enjoyed this book and think others may also benefit from the information contained within then why not leave an honest review on the sales page so that hopefully others may also benefit and overcome their approach anxiety.

I really do wish you the best of luck. Remember, I've been there, I know exactly how you feel and believe me, it gets easier and that's when the fun begins.

Charlie Valentino

Also By Charlie Valentino

First Date Tips For Men

Confidence For Men

Meet Women On Facebook

2295147R00029

Printed in Great Britain
by Amazon.co.uk, Ltd.,
Marston Gate.